IN CASE OF RAIN

In Case of Rain

When Faith is Challenged by Life

Susan Anderson

RESOURCE *Publications* · Eugene, Oregon

IN CASE OF RAIN
When Faith is Challenged by Life

Resource Publications
An Imprint of Wipf and Stock Publishers
199 W. 8th Ave., Suite 3
Eugene, OR 97401

www.wipfandstock.com

PAPERBACK ISBN: 978-1-5326-9230-7
HARDCOVER ISBN: 978-1-5326-9231-4
EBOOK ISBN: 978-1-5326-9232-1

Manufactured in the U.S.A.   AUGUST 1, 2019

Contents

Introduction | vii

Incredible Truth | 1
Little to Lose | 3
The Father's Voice | 5
Yesterday, So Long Ago | 6
Memories | 7
Reflection: Treasure in the Field | 9
My Old Cross | 10
Always to Worship | 12
Will Anyone Hear? | 14
A Gentle Touch | 15
Reflection: Together | 17
The Reason To Go On | 18
A Clear Path | 20
Illusions of Defeat | 21
Reflection: Hope | 23
The Kiss | 24
Miles Away, Years Apart | 25
The Traveler | 26

A Second Chance | 28
Today | 29
The Thief | 31
A Time Away | 33
An Ode to Stuff | 35
An Ode to Monday | 37
An Unexpected Place | 39
All For Us | 42
Arising | 44
Friday Faces | 46
Reflection: DNA | 49
The Temptation | 50
Reflection: After the Fall | 56
The Story of Job | 57
Reflection: The Children of Saturday | 66
The Story of Jonah | 68
Reflection: The Favor of God | 75
An Essay: Up From the Valley | 77

Introduction

It is my hope and prayer that this little book will encourage you and remind you of the love, the mercy and the power of our God. I have written these poems and essays over many years. He has brought me through difficult days, days of rain. And now I know that when hard times come, Jesus will see me through.

May you come through your days of rain and see the sun shine once again, resting in God's love for you. He knows your name, He knows your heart, He knows your pain—and He cares.

Let the Son rise.

This is my favorite poem. I wrote it after seeing the awe- inspiring night sky in northern Maine, and considering our amazing God who created it—and the smallness of myself.

Incredible Truth

Psalm 8:3, 4

When I consider your heavens, the work of your fingers, the moon and stars which you have set in place, what is man that you are mindful of him, the son of man that you care for him?

In all the vast expanse of space
With endless stars in ordered courses,
Where countless planets are birthed and die,
Never seen by human eyes,
In all the glorious variety
Of gas and light and air and earth
Fashioning the tapestry of the sky,
Who am I?

Upon this tiny dot of dust
Where billions have come and lived and gone
In a span of minute brevity,
With eternity behind and yet to be,
Where kings and kingdoms rose and fell
And greatness reached by precious few
Among the masses of history,
What of me?

A dot upon this dot of dust,
One of billions in endless array
Who has earned no greatness, won no fame,
A hidden player of a tiny game,
Lost in the breadth of time and numbers
Of no possible consequence.
Yet the incredible truth remains:
He knows my name!
   He knows my name!

When you're discouraged and nothing seems to work, why not reach out to the One who offers hope? That was what the woman in Mark 5:25-29 decided. She had been sick for so long. And now there was a chance . . .

Little to Lose

Isaiah 55:6

Seek the Lord while he may be found; call upon him while he is near.

Have I the strength to leave this place,
To find Thee who they say can heal?
And while I seek You, could I face
The fear and dread the crowd would feel?

It is against the law for me
To touch who are considered whole.
Do I dare defy decree,
And spread uncleanness to my soul?

Should I risk all on what I've heard?
Dare I believe that it is true?
My heart cries out to trust the words,
And I have little else to lose.

For all is spent, all has been lost.
Man's knowledge holds no hope for me.
Now shall I pay the final cost,
And spend my only hope on Thee?

If only half is true of what they say,
That at Your touch the blind can see
And by Your command the storm obeyed,
Then perhaps there still is hope for me.

So while You're here within our shores
I'll cast aside the nagging doubts
And trust You're able to restore
Those who are willing to reach out.

You needn't turn your face to mine,
You mustn't touch one such as me.
I can just follow from behind
And touch the cloth that touches Thee.

God never tires of calling out to us.
His voice, His hand, is ever there, waiting for us to respond.

The Father's Voice

Revelation 3:20

Here I am! If anyone hears my voice and opens the door, I will come in
and eat with him and he with me.

Through all the din of daily routine
As your busy days peel away precious years
And your hours are filled with the clutter of life,
The Father's voice is calling.
Through the noise of work and play,
In the midst of all the voices
Of children, of friends, of strangers,
There is one voice that is different,
And it is calling out your name.
Whether or not you stop to listen.
Whether or not you care to hear.
Like the ticking of a clock.
Like the beating of a heart.
Like the rhythm of the ocean waves.
Continual, unending, untiring.
Just as gentle,
Just as loving,
Just as if He knew you'd answer.

To my beautiful, loving daughter, Sara. She spent her life in a wheelchair, but her spirit soared, unrestrained. She passed away in 1989 at seventeen. Even at that young age, she touched many people's lives with the love of Jesus.

Yesterday, So Long Ago

Proverbs 14:13

Even in laughter the heart may ache, and joy may end in grief.

It's been many years—a lifetime ago.
Yet I can still see her face so clearly;
The summertime freckles that she hated & I loved,
The long dark hair drawn up and tied.
I can see those large eyes lit with laughter,
And so many times shiny with tears, mixing with my own.
My mother-ears can hear her sweet song, her easy laugh,
Her chatting, her praying, her crying.
I remember the pain she bore,
And the all-inclusive love that entered a room with her
And stayed behind as she wheeled away
Like the lingering scent of sweet perfume.
She is embedded in my heart, frozen in time,
Untarnished and pure.
She will never change.
Little is left of the person I was then,
Except for that bubble in my heart which holds her memory,
Safe, unchanging, sweet and aching.
Full of love, full of pain.

Memories—good or bad—can be traps. We need to be aware of their power over our lives. Remember, yes. But go on from there to see and live for today.

Memories

Psalm 40:2,3

He set my feet on a rock and gave me a firm place to stand. He put a new song in my mouth.

There is a room within each heart
Where memories are stored away,
And frequent visits there will have
Profound effects on life today.

Memories we choose to handle often,
Be they ones of joy or sorrow,
Stale the freshness of today
And bring the past into tomorrow.

Like colored glass before our eyes
They tint our vision of what is now.
And hope is limited in scope
To what those colors will allow.

Then there are those memories
Hidden in a corner, where
Cloaked with dust and tied secure,
They're never touched, but always there.

Never brought into the light,
They grow within the darkest part,
'Till they break free and start to fill
The other rooms within our heart.

No longer only memories,
Now they live within today;
Still not opened, still not touched,
Yet always there to block our way.

But there will come a point in time
When we must choose to be set free,
And remove the roadblocks of our past
Or live entombed by memories.

And that's when we can ask the Lord,
The One we know that we can trust,
To walk beside as we go through
The fearful rooms of dark and dust.

He'll go with us into each place
And shine within the darkest parts,
So we may see them in His light
And clear away our cluttered hearts.

Free to live a day that's new!
The voices of the past are stilled!
Those things which once had blocked our way,
Now blocks that can be used to build.

Want to go treasure hunting? Careful—you might be taking on more than you thought!

Reflection: Treasure in the Field

Matthew 13:44

"The kingdom of heaven is like treasure hidden in a field. When a man found it, he hid it again, and then in his joy went and sold all he had and bought that field . . ."

In the beginning of this parable, the field holding the treasure did not belong to the man. But, obviously, he was searching for the treasure. It was hidden and he had to look to find it. *Those who seek God, find Him.*

Scripture often compares the world to a field (Mt. 13:38 for example—"The field is the world . . ."). The man didn't buy the treasure. He bought the field, and the treasure came with it. We cannot obtain the Kingdom without investing in the world (the people). (John 3:16: "God so loved the world.") We have to invest what we have (time, talents, resources, care) in people if we are to obtain the treasure of the Kingdom. We must understand the value that God places on the world, the people that He loves. *That's where He put His treasure!*

That is why "faith without works is dead". It's like trying to buy the treasure without the field. It doesn't work, because you can't take the treasure out of the field. God put it there for a reason.

Once the man in the parable saw the value and bought the field, he had no more resources of his own, just the treasure. So he would have to use the resources of the treasure in order to plow the field, plant a crop or build a home. All would come from the treasure. All of what we need to do God's work in this world, to show the love of Jesus, comes from God, from His Spirit working in us. *That's the treasure!*

*We can allow the burden of a problem or handicap or persistent diffi-
culty to become our identity, to define or revoke our goals. We feel brave,
tackling it alone instead of giving the burden of it, the mental weight of
it, to God and allowing Him to lift the yoke of worry and onus, permit-
ting us to find a way forward.*

My Old Cross

Psalm 68:19

Praise be to the Lord, to God our Savior, who daily bears our burdens.

It lay at my feet now—that cross—my cross,
The one I was not meant to bear, but chose to carry.
It was built by my own hands
With the material of circumstance and trials.

I thought it was my portion,
My lot, to carry this cross.
And I bore it well for a time
With the strength that youth can lend.

Clutched solidly before me,
It became oddly comforting with the passing of years.
For who would I be without it?
And what would be my purpose?

It had become my shield against change,
My weapon against growth,
My excuse for allowing dreams to remain only dreams.
I had allowed my burden to become my friend.

But strength fails over time,
When the road is steep and the weight heavy.
And the day came when I could carry it no longer.
When I knew I must either release it, or fall with it.

With desperation and weakness now stronger than the fear,
Came the willingness to let go.
And with that willingness came the freedom to finally hear
What had always been true.

And now my old cross lies where it had always belonged -
At the foot of another, much heavier cross,
Where He who bore this one,
Will also bear mine.

There are days when worship seems impossible or hypocritical, because of what's going on in life. But God is God, no matter what the circumstances. You can worship Him for being the Creator of the universe, for fashioning a rose or coloring a sunset, or creating the miracle of a newborn baby . . .

Always to Worship

Revelation 14:7b

Worship him who made the heavens, the earth, the sea and the springs of water.

I sat and watched the others worship
But I could not enter in.
I listened to songs of praise and thanksgiving
But could find no reason for thankfulness.

And during that painful and troubled time
I saw a truth that will not fade -
A truth that now allows me to take part,
That supersedes the truth of life around me:

I can't always worship from a joyful heart,
But I can always worship Him for who He is.
I can't always praise Him for the way my life is going,
But I can always praise Him for being Almighty God.

For when I can't rejoice, He is still God.
And when life is hard, He is still the Creator of all.
And nothing can make Him less than who He is.
Reasons enough to worship, reasons enough to praise.

And when the current troubles subside
And my soul is again aligned with my will,
I know that joy will return to my song
And thanksgiving to my worship.

Do we listen to people—I mean really listen? Or do we simply use their words as a platform for our own ideas and words? Sometimes all people need is someone to hear their heart.

Will Anyone Hear?

James 1:19a

. . . Everyone should be quick to listen, slow to speak

One might think that you were listening,
Because you were not the one speaking.
But the words in your mind were yours, not mine –
Those that would be said when I was done,
Or when enough time passed between the pockets of noise.

One might think that you had heard my heart
For we were close enough to reach and touch.
But my cry was barely a whisper,
No match for the roar of experience and wisdom.
And you touched me only to highlight your truth.

I know you meant your words as a kindness,
Your direction and good judgment as a help.
But that is not what I longed for today.
Just for now I wanted truth to give way to mercy,
And wisdom be put aside in favor of kindness.

Today I simply needed someone to hear,
Finding the strength that I am not alone
Because a friend was willing to listen
To a heart not yet ready to mend.
And then perhaps, in time, *we would sit again.*

Often we speak too quickly, not appreciating the power of our words. No apology can erase words once spoken; and regret is a cruel companion.

A Gentle Touch

First Peter 3:4

. . . the unfailing beauty of a gentle and quiet spirit which is of great worth in God's sight.

We save our softest touches,
Using them sparingly
On a baby's cheek,
On the petals of a rose,
On a stem of a fine crystal glass.

We are so very careful
Not to hurt or mar or break,
For we value the fragile beauty
And would not be the one
To harm such things.

We understand that they
Have no defense against
A harsh stroke or careless touch,
And once damaged
Will remain so.

But hearts are as fragile
As a newborn's cheek,
Easier to tear than petals of a rose,
As readily broken
As a fine crystal glass.

God has placed in our lives
The hearts of those around us,
Hearts much like our own,
Fragile and sensitive to
The touch of our words.

Do we value their beauty,
Knowing that God prizes all hearts?
Do we see the need for carefulness?
Or do we correct with harsh appraisal
A heart not beating in tandem with ours?

These were placed in our hand
For safekeeping
By a God of gentle touches,
Who trusts us to handle with care
That which is dear to Him.

From the mouth of one
To the heart of another.
Let us spend our softest touches
On the fragile hearts of others
With words of grace and hope.

Remembering that our hearts, too,
Are held in another's hand.

Reflection: Together

New England, The Cradle of Liberty, where that value was won for all our generations. Where people worked together, decided together, prayed together, fought and died together, and ultimately prevailed together as our shared freedom became the foundation of "one nation under God".

But somewhere along our road we have forgotten freedom's meaning and the way it was attained. Now independence means aloneness, and liberty is equated with personal privilege. We wear self-sufficiency as a badge of honor, something to have our sons and daughters aspire to. We have forgotten that it was not one pen, not one idea, not one gun, not one prayer, not one grave—only one God.

We need to realize again the power of together, the need for each other, the thought that what you can do combined with what I can do can accomplish what I alone cannot. We need to trade the promise of individual praise and solitary accomplishment in favor of a far larger purpose where the goal is to love, and the praise goes to God, and the prize is eternal liberty and everlasting freedom for all those who care to come.

It was together that we worked to build a nation here. Let it be together that we work to establish His Kingdom here.

There are times in life that are filled with trouble and heartache—times when we question our faith. God does not promise us freedom from trouble, only freedom from bitterness and hopelessness, if we are willing to let it go.

The Reason To Go On

Jeremiah 29:11

I know the plans I have for you, declares the Lord, plans to prosper you and not to harm you, plans to give you hope and a future.

On those dark nights which come to us all
When dreams would be a cherished relief from reality
And my mind replays troubles as a remorseless drum,
The thought reappears, "Perhaps it is time to walk away."

When prayers fall like rocks as they leave my lips,
And my spirit cannot climb over the wall of my soul,
When questions have no answers, or answers no hope,
I think I cannot continue, because I don't understand.

But then, as always, the thought can go no further.
For the ageless question follows, "Where else would I go?"
I have been the other way, with no truth, no substance.
My heart would not permit it; it is no longer an option.

And can I stay in this place and not continue,
Planting myself as a stubborn child before my Father?
Shall I demand understanding and freedom from trouble?
Is my pain special, surpassing that of others?

No. My only claim to specialness lies in my Father's heart.
I am special because of His love for me, His plan for me.
And that is why, you see, there is no other path for me.
It's the reason to walk this way, the reason to go on.

How to live life—the choices we all must make, some mundane, others frightfully important.

A Clear Path

Psalm 48:14

For this God is our God forever and ever; He will be our guide even to the end.

I prayed for a clear path, a sure way.
I prayed that God would define my direction,
That I would not doubt once the choice was made.
I longed for that indefinable "knowing",
And the peace that comes from seeing clearly.

It seemed to me a good prayer, a right prayer,
A prayer both spiritual and practical
For a time when change was at hand.
I wanted to choose the way that would please Him,
Knowing that it would also be the best for me.

But now I see that the best for me is uncertainty,
And what I must long for is not a knowing, but a trusting,
Not a map, but a guide.
For peace does not come from seeing the path clearly,
But from seeing clearly the One who knows the way.

"And the winner is . . ." Really?

Illusions of Defeat

Isaiah 53:11a

After the suffering of his soul, he will see the light of life and be
satisfied.

How do you recognize defeat?
What does it look like?
What signs indicate its presence?

Tears? Loss? Weakness, perhaps?
Misfortune or distress?
Would suffering tell you?
Would injury or failure be its mark?

How quick we are to cry defeat
For ourselves and for others.
How obvious the victor!
How conspicuous the loser!

But what is apparent,
May not in truth be so.
For our eyes may tell one story
While the Spirit tells another.

How obvious it must have seemed
To those standing at the foot of the Cross
That defeat belonged to the sufferer,
To the weak one, to the dying.

There were tears and distress,
Injuries to both body and soul.
The man, to all appearances,
Was a failure, a supreme disappointment.

Yet never was a victory more complete,
Never a triumph more perfect
For all men, for all time
Than the one purchased by that death.

But we have an enemy
Who desires us to embrace defeat,
That we may yield our weapons
And quit the battle.

Do not be deceived by his cries of failure.
Don't be deterred by the appearance of things.
Do not yield your sword
Or remove the armor.

For what we see with our eyes
May only be the illusion of defeat
On the very threshold of victory.

There is a big difference between wishing and hoping.

Reflection: Hope

Hebrews 11:1

"Now faith is being sure of what we hope for, and certain of what we do not see."

Faith needs hopes. You need a hope to apply faith to. Where there are no hopes, faith is unnecessary.

The dictionary defines hope: "To wish for something, with expectation of its fulfillment." It defines a wish as: "A desire or longing for something."

Where there are no hopes, there can be *belief*, but not an *active faith*. Hope attracts faith to itself in order to move toward the fulfillment of the expectation. Wishes do not have an expectation of fulfillment. They are dreams.

Romans 5:4 says that suffering produces perseverance, which produces character, which produces hope. Hope comes out of our character formed by experience. Hope isn't an immature thing— quite the opposite.

Sometimes there are things in our lives that we greatly desire to do or to become, but we look at ourselves and see no expectation of fulfillment. They are only wishes. And they will remain wishes until we are able to remember what God has already done and know that He is *with* us and *for* us and can *make the difference.* And that's when the wish attracts faith to itself and turns into a hope! When that happens, the perseverance will come as the joy of expectation of its fulfillment sets our heart to the task ahead.

I often have to ask myself if I am wishing or hoping. It makes all the difference in the world.

There seems to be no end to what this world purports to offer. Things, stuff, fun, indulgence, wealth, etc. Beware—it comes with a price.

The Kiss

Joshua 24:15b

Choose for yourselves this day whom you will serve.

Who has had such a friend as the world,
A friend of such wisdom and pleasure?
Who has more to offer than he?
And who does not want what he can give?

"Come with me!" he calls to young and old.
"Come and see and feel and taste and touch."
So we run here and there, seeing and wanting,
With no boundary between need and desire.

And that which we touch is never enough.
For as it comes to our hand, we are shown yet another.
"You do not have this one!" he cries in our ears.
And dutifully we rush to that which we lack.

And when the short years of our running are over
And we stand at the beginning of eternity,
We receive our friend's parting embrace.
The kiss of the world.
The Judas kiss.

God is full of surprises and plans we do not know. His timing is always perfect! My best friend, my sister, MaryAnn. Ten years younger, she was only ten years old when I was off on my own.

Miles Away, Years Apart

James 4:14a

You don't know what will happen tomorrow.

I would have chosen to be there
As you went from child to woman.
I would have chosen fewer years between us,
Fewer miles between our homes.
I would have chosen to know you then,
To have been your confidant, your friend.

But the Lord chose a different way.
He chose our friendship for these days,
To connect us as women, as equals.
We come as who we are now,
Without labels of who we were;
Our connection not with shared memories,
But with a shared heart.
The miles and years now enrich,
Each giving to the other a new way to see life.

Now I am glad it has gone this way.
The Lord knew I would need a friend,
Right now, in these later years.
And who would have thought
That she would have been there all along—
Miles away and years apart . . .

Sometimes people (especially young people) doubt God's way and choose to go down a different road. It is risky. Love them without judgment, and pray for them. They can return, stronger for the experience.

The Traveler

Jeremiah 6:16

Stand at the crossroads and look . . . ask where the good way is, and walk in it.

So restless and unsure.
So disordered and doubting.
Searching so hard for something
Which was always there beside.

How far down must you go
Before you are willing to look up?
How far will you wander
Before you dream again of home?
How many strangers must you see
Before you call to mind your Father's face?

Have you yet sensed the unreality
Of the freedom which you seek?
Have the pleasures of the moment
Begun to ring hollow?
Have you felt the sense that something's wrong
As you pursue your dream of freedom?

Take care, my traveler, not to go too far
That you forget your way;
Not to drift so long
That you do not remember.

For strangers amuse, but they do not love;
Illusion is poor substitute for truth;
And true freedom is not a dream, but a path.

Surprisingly, the medical test said that I had a future. Surprisingly, in spite of all my life's difficulties, I found that I wanted that future.

A Second Chance

Second Samuel 22:17

He reached down from on high and took hold of me. He drew me out of deep waters.

I've been given a second chance,
A gift to dream again,
Another door to open, new thing to try.
A chance to stay for a little while longer
And see to those things left undone.

I have a chance to do life better,
To capture a piece of who He meant for me to be,
Of what He meant for me to do.
To take what is left and continue on
With purpose and with hope.

It is time to leave this endless valley.
Leave its language, its mindset, its tedium,
And breathe the air of the hillside,
Where words have hope, and minds have plans
And challenges hold promise.

I don't believe that God wants our lives to be a dull repetition of days, but days with purpose and newness and possibilities. Are we open to see it?

Today

First Corinthians 9:24b

... Run in such a way as to get the prize.

I always thought of today as the next step of yesterday
And watched each stride with a critical eye,
Attention focused on my feet and the uneven ground.

Careful not to stumble, I would seldom glance up
To see what I was passing by or what may lie ahead,
For I assumed it would simply be more of the same.

I expected little more of myself or of life today
Than what was realized last week or last year;
The passage of time noticed only in seasons and in children.

And so tomorrow, you see, held little promise,
Except another stride along the perilous path –
A step like the last one—and the one before.

I think now about all the years that I have walked,
Sad for what I may have missed during the journey
In an effort to keep from falling, from failing.

Being vigilant for missteps, I had ignored the view.
I saw the rocks, but not the signs of possibilities.
My step was more sure, but the walk uninspiring.

How much better it would have been to fall now and then,
Tending to my wounds or mistakes along an exciting road,
Daring to try, daring to fail, finding the path meant just for me!

I see now that I would have risked nothing by looking up.
For no matter how people walk, they will stumble and fall.
How much better to heal with expectancy of what could be!

Although my way is shorter now, I will change my focus.
I will look up from my feet to see the flavor of today,
And the chance that it holds within its hours a new thing.

Do not wait as long as I to see the signs of opportunity.
Yesterday's echo need not be your today.
Look up, and walk, and fall, and heal, and walk again tomorrow.
For Destiny does not lie at our feet.

The story of a man I knew, who allowed hurt to rule his thoughts and life.

The Thief

Hebrews 12:15

See to it that no one misses the grace of God and that no bitter root
grows up to cause trouble

Once upon a recent time
(As all proper stories start)
There was a good and pleasant man
With a kind and gentle heart.

Many sought to be his friend
For with him found a partner true,
A listening ear and tender words,
Qualities possessed by few.

But hearts like his wound easily
By thoughtless word or careless deed.
And injuries are hard to heal
If not attended to with speed.

And within a multitude of friends
The danger's sure to multiply
That one will say or do a thing
Which cause a bit of heart to die.

And this good and pleasant man
Turned from seeking to be healed.
He set his mind upon his wound,
And built around himself a shield.

And as the months and years went by
He kept himself alone, apart;
As injustice turned to bitterness
That formed a root within his heart.

Men no longer sought him out
For he refused to be consoled.
And though some would recall his name
None knew again his gentle soul.

There is no thief as unforgiveness
Who steals away the hearts of men,
Turns to stone what once was soft,
And forms a stranger from a friend.

*Ahh vacations! Rest! What a balm for the body and soul! Just a few
hours away in Quebec City, I and my friend found that wonderful rest.*

A Time Away

Hebrews 4:9, 10

There remains a rest for the people of God; for anyone who enters
God's rest also rests from his own work, just as God did from his.

A time away. Seeing different things through refocused eyes.
Sighing as the warmth of an evening breeze
Washes over a newly relaxed body.
A small veranda offers a view of housetops and the river beyond.
On the table is a bottle of wine and torn pieces of crusty bread.
We are welcome outsiders here,
From whom nothing is expected, nothing required.

The narrow streets are old, with conjoined homes,
Boundaried only by color and ownership.
Weathered windows of the houses are opened outward,
The residents unconcerned that they are seen or heard,
For here the warm breezes are prized and short-lived.
Too soon these windows will be locked and glazed with ice.

We walk slowly down the unfamiliar streets
That lead to shops and artists' displays
Where touchable memories can be purchased.
People in the sidewalk cafes speak in low tones,
The foreign words flowing in a charming stream,
Like an unintelligible concert.

Street performers and sidewalk musicians vie for attention,
Their talents worth more than the coins in their cases.
An old stone church attracts visitors but not worshippers,
Its purpose replaced by a small souvenir shop behind the pews.
Around a bend, the breeze carries an enticing aroma
Which has escaped from an open bakery door.
We find no reason to fight the temptation.

A new day brings a new adventure
As a bridge ushers us onto a magical island of farms and fields.
We see a cluster of cows grazing lazily, apathetic to our presence.
At the end of a meadow, an aged stone house with a yellow door
Is silhouetted against the water beyond.
It seems an unreal place, an idyllic rendering,
As if we had stepped between the pages of a lovely old book.

And now back home where all things are familiar,
And the days are much the same, holding few surprises,
I am content to know that I had been to another place.
And a smile of remembrance can be had by
The smell of wine, the tang of cheese,
Or a figure in an open window, catching a summer breeze.

Just how much stuff do we need??? Apparently, always more.

An Ode to Stuff

Revelation 21:5

I am making everything new!

Here's to our things—our junk—our stuff!
No matter how much, there's never enough.
There's stuff in our drawers, stuff in our closets,
And empty containers for future deposits.

We've got stuff in the attic and in the garage,
Jumbled together, the small with the large.
Broken or useless, in bags without measure,
Kept for the time one will think it a treasure.

What is it with *stuff* that we hold it so dear,
That we cram it in there and jam it in here?
Our children share rooms until they are grown,
But most family's stuff has a room of its own!

The heap we amass in our own life's duration,
We solemnly bequeath to the next generation;
Who will stack up that stuff to such dizzying height
That just walking by it would give one a fright!

How was the thought born upon this good Earth
That the sum of our stuff is our measure of worth,
That all that we are is all that we own?
How very far from the truth we have grown!

Is it stuff that will save us? Can it forgive?
Does it validate the life that we live?
Can the contents of bags and boxes and closets
Affect the way God looks upon us?

Was He seeing this weakness, had He a clue,
When He said that in Heaven, "All things will be *new*!"?
When our time here is ended, surely it will be clear
That our stuff is just junk—and we'll leave it all here!

An Ode to Monday

Ecclesiastes 3:13

That everyone may eat and drink and find satisfaction in all his toil— this is the gift of God.

And now it is Monday, the start of the week,
When we question the wisdom of that which we seek.
When the rat race begins at 8 sharp, if you please.
(At least a rat would be getting some cheese.)

In a blink of an eye the weekend was done,
But Monday makes up for that—and then some.
The day that crap happens at such regular pace
You think you can't possibly finish the race.

What is it about these twenty-four hours
That gives it such incredible powers
To frustrate and anger, upset and control
And turn a pleasant person like me to a troll?

Could it be that it's just a regular day—
That the problem lies with me in a way?
I don't like to think so, but maybe it's true,
That Mondays serve a good purpose or two.

To appreciate heaven we must peek into hell;
To get to the peanut, we must break through the shell.
Maybe Sundays would not be considered so fair
If Mondays weren't coming 'round to compare!

So thank God for Mondays, be tornado or breeze;
May I deal with the crap in a way that would please.
And if You see fit, as I push through the bends,
May this rat find a small piece of cheese at the end.

Christmas, like no other time of year, fills us with great and varied emotions. And beneath all the activity and distractions, it can touch our hearts in surprising ways.

An Unexpected Place

Isiah 9:6a

For unto us a child is born, unto us a son is given . . .

What are you looking for this Christmas,
Among the boxes wrapped and bowed?
What are you expecting to find inside?
Will it be what you supposed?

Or will the gift not be the thing
On which you set your heart and mind;
What you expected, what you hoped,
What you thought that you would find?

What are you looking for this Christmas,
When family comes from all around
To be together on this day when
Expectation, irritation, obligation all abound?

Do you hope that this Noel
Will paint the perfect Christmas scene
Of loving family, jolly friends
Singing carols by the tree?

Well, most of us will find a mix
Of disappointment and delight,
Formed by traditions, fed by stories
Of that holy, silent night.

On the first of Christmases
For three men who traveled far
There were expectations too
When they were following a star.

They knew it was the Lord of Lords'
The Savior's star that guided them.
And so they came with expectations
To see a King in Bethlehem.

Imagine for a moment what they thought
When at last they reached the town.
What they expected to see that Christmas
Was nothing like what they had found.

They expected a throne, and found a trough.
Followed a light to discover a cave.
Their gifts of gold lay in the straw.
They searched for a King, but encountered a Babe.

And in that unexpected place,
As humble as one would allow,
They touched the very heart of God
Embodied in a little Child.

They found what they were seeking
In that unlikely, holy site.
They saw the Savior of the world,
The Babe who would become the Light!

And for centuries the story's told
Of how they by a star were led,
How they sought the King of Israel
And found Him in a manger bed.

While all across the countryside
On that same night of hope and grace,
Were people filled with sad despair,
Living through hard and sorrowful days.

Had they only raised their heads
They could have seen the hopeful light.
They could have followed where it led.
They could have known the joy that night.

They could have touched the Son of God
For the star shone bright for everyone!
But three were seeking, three pursuing,
And three would see what God had done.

What are you looking for this Christmas?
Can it be found beneath a tree?
Will expectations be unfulfilled
With gifts or friends or family?

And will you settle for that circumstance
Or will you dare to raise your eyes;
To look higher, to seek further
To find the only perfect prize?

For the Light that led the wise men
Can lead you by His grace,
To touch the very heart of God
In some *unexpected* place.

When I think of the nativity, it amazes me the way in which our Almighty God chose to come to us.

All For Us

Philippians 2:6-8

Who, being in very nature God, did not consider equality with God something to be grasped, but made himself nothing, taking the very nature of a servant, being made in human likeness. And being found in appearance as a man, he humbled himself and became obedient to death . . .

He could have come in a display of glory on that first Christmas,
With angels trumpeting His arrival.
He could have ridden to earth atop billowing clouds
That He Himself had created.
He could have worn robes of gold and a crown of jewels—
For it is He who speaks their splendor into being.
He could have commanded that every star burn with new intensity,
Or every star drop from heaven, and He Himself be the only light.
There was no one higher to command mercy.
There was no demand on Him for gentleness.

The only grounds for humility was grace.
The only reason for meekness was love.
The stable, the mother and father, the child of flesh and blood,
The tidings of good news to lowly men,
The one star that shone brightly for those who were seeking,
Tell us of the character of our God.

He did not come to condemn, though it would have been His right.
He did not come in power, though all authority was His.
He came with grace and forgiveness.
He came with kindness and love.
He came to offer us life with purpose.
He still does.

When our hearts are quiet before Him, we can touch our God
As the shepherds did when they knelt by His bed.
When He seems far away, we need only to follow the light
That He Himself placed within us,
And we will find Him as the wise men did.
And should we pray as Mary, giving her life to His purpose,
We too will give birth—to forgiveness and kindness and love
That will fill the world in which we live.

Come to Bethlehem this Christmas.
Be one who beholds the Christ child.
Come from places far from him and find light without judgment.
Come and discover the mighty God who became a child
So that we could see, and touch, and know Him.
From the straw of His bed, to the wood of His cross,
His life here was for us—His mortality was for us.
God's gift, wrapped in swaddling clothes.
Come, let us adore Him!

Easter—celebrating the day Christ shared the greatest of all victories with us, so that we can take hold and participate in the hope that this day brings.

Arising

Ephesians 2:6

And God raised us up with Christ and seated us with him in the heavenly realms . . .

And on the third day He arose.
He arose from the dreadful Friday of pain.
He arose from the time of suffering and aloneness.
He arose from rejection, from betrayal, from death.
He arose that day from the snare of hell itself.

But on that third day, He did not arise into Heaven.
He did not at once arise to the throne beside his Father.
He arose first to earth—He arose to us.
He arose to the rejecters and betrayers,
To the believers and the doubters and the disheartened.

He did not appear to the king of the land
Who had given the order for His suffering and death.
He did not go to the halls of the powerful men
Who had Him killed to protect their positions.
He felt no need to display His power before them.

He appeared to women who had come to His tomb with tears.
He walked along a road, talking with discouraged men.
He appeared to his overjoyed friends and sat and ate with them.
He went to the seashore, and blessed the fishermen's catch.
The Risen Savior walked again in the footsteps of the carpenter's Son.

The third day was not for the powerful and mighty of earth.
It was not for the purpose of retribution.
It was not to seize authority from evil systems.
But it was to give hope and assurance to ordinary people.
Hope for this life and the assurance of God's love and provision.

Now we can know that from a dreadful day of pain—*we* can arise.
That from a time of suffering and aloneness—*we* can arise.
That from rejection and betrayal—*we* can arise.
We have only to reach out and take the nail-pierced hand,
The hand of Mary's son, the sacrificed Lamb, the Risen Lord.

The Crucifixion. All the players were there—each with his/her thoughts and feelings about this monumental event that would change everything for all time.

Friday Faces

Luke 23:48

When all the people who had gathered to witness this sight saw what took place, they beat their breasts and went away. But all those who knew Him stood at a distance, including the women who followed Him from Galilee, watching these things.

The faces of Friday.
Around the courtyard, along the road, on the hill,
Watching the scene unfolding before them -
Each reflecting their part in the story.

The face of a soldier, detesting the foul but familiar work.
This is not his affair, this is not his king.
He frowns as he wipes the blood from his hand.
Just another day.

The face of a priest, annoyed at the disturbing events
Which caused this day to be necessary.
He looks with approval at his robed reflection.
An unfortunate day.

The face of a governor, tense and anxious.
He had washed his hands of responsibility,
But he cannot cleanse his mind.
A day of guilt.

The face of a prostitute, lost in powerless frustration.
The only kindness she knew, she is helpless to return.
She bemoans the weakness of her womanhood.
A day of loss.

The face of a fisherman, streaked with tears of shame
For courage that failed him and failed his Lord.
His words are impossible to erase.
A day of regret.

The face of a thief, eyes wide with fear and dread
Lamenting the errors and actions that brought him here.
His life will soon be over.
A day of judgment.

The face of a mother, frozen in horror,
Straining against hands that are holding her back
From running to her suffering son.
A day of grief.

And in the midst, the face of the carpenter's son,
Wet with His own blood—forsaken, reviled,
Struggling with the pain that is His chosen destiny.
A day of agony and mortality. A day of redemption.

None but the sufferer knows
That the story and purpose is not ending here;
That with the pain, misery and darkness of Friday,
He is purchasing a Sunday.

The fisherman, the mother, the thief, the prostitute
Will not be left in their place of sorrow,
But will see with their own eyes their living hope.
They will become—the faces of Sunday.

And now we know that within the dark Fridays of our lives,
Amid the grief, or regret, or loss, or shame
Or in the uncertainty and dimness of Saturdays,
There is the incredible hope, the bright promise
That Sunday will come.

Reflection: DNA

The Bible says that we are redeemed by the blood of Jesus. That always puzzled me. Why not say the *death* of Jesus? Why the blood? It seems so . . . I don't know . . . violent?

So I thought a lot about it, did some studying, and though I certainly don't purport to understand it all, a little light, one piece of the puzzle, did come.

Science has learned a lot the last 20 years about blood, how it is the blueprint of who we are, genetically speaking. They can trace back and tell who your father or mother is or was, if they have a sample of their blood. Each of us are the product of the blood of our father and the blood of our mother, together.

So, imagine—just for a moment—what the DNA of Jesus' blood would have held! I believe it would have included the very essence of God, the substance of holiness and purity and power. And it held the essence of Mary, a regular, common woman. That blood of Jesus held the blueprint of God and woman—together!

The blood of Jesus held within it the story of salvation—of God coming to us. What an incredible, precious thing! The merging of *God and man.* It is not surprising to me now that it holds within it the power to purify, to redeem.

Violent? Oh no. Very much the opposite. It is love and compassion. It is God's desire to call us His children.

What was the conversation like between Eve and the serpent in the Garden of Eden? If she could speak to us today, what might she tell us of that first temptation, how she felt and what she thought? And what advice might she offer?

Here is one possibility . . .

The Temptation

1 Corinthians 10:13b

But when you are tempted, God will also provide a way out so that you can stand up under it.

"I cannot eat of this tree," I said.
"I cannot eat, or I shall die."
And with knowing eyes and wizened grin,
He said that I believed a lie.

"Die—from this? From harmless fruit?
Does it appear that it would kill?
Study closely—then discard it
If you think it harmful still.

But is it not a perfect fruit,
Superior to all?" he cried,
"Lovely to look at and to touch.
In such a thing, could death reside?

Don't you know that evil's held
In things unpleasant to the eyes?
But beauty holds the precious hope
Of all the things that man would prize.

Do I seem weak to you, or ill?
For your proof just look and see.
I live within these branches, yet
No evil has befallen me!"

And as I listened, I could feel
The seed of doubt that had been sown.
And desire for that which was forbidden
Warred with truth that I had known.

Had I the wisdom then to run,
To leave temptation far behind
And trust the warning of my King,
Then paradise would still be mine.

But wisdom was the one to flee.
And as thoughts conflicted in my head,
The question rightly posed to God
I asked the serpent here instead.

"All things were given unto us.
All things for our use, but one.
Why would my Lord forbid us this
If by its taste no harm is done?"

"Because" he said, his eyes ablaze.
"He knows the power hidden there.
Wisdom for those who would partake.
And that, you see, He will not share.

It's true that on the day you eat
All he knows will be your own,
Good and evil, right and wrong.
And wisdom lets you stand alone.

You were created in His likeness,
In most ways a true reflection.
But there is one thing your image lacks
And knowledge brings it to perfection.

With just one bite you become as He!
At a single stroke you are His peer!
No more children to be taught
For you will be His equal here!

A glorious and noble goal
To ascend up to a higher place!
And rise to where you could not reach
If dependent on another's grace."

"Cast aside the serpent's words,"
My heart cried, "for they are wrong!"
But lies take root in little time,
And I had listened much too long.

Questions thundered in my mind
And ambition rose to lofty heights.
The truth lay on the ground, discarded
For clouds of lies had dimmed my sight.

Is knowledge evil, a thing to reject?
Would not the prize be worth the trying?
Is desire to be like my Lord wrong?
What would the serpent gain from lying?

Could death grow in this perfect garden?
Did not the Lord create this tree?
And if I aspire to be like Him,
Would He not think well of me?

Hands trembling in expectation,
I raised it to my lips and ate.
The decision made, the die was cast.
I turned and shared it with my mate.

With sweet taste still upon our tongues,
The promised burst of knowledge came.
But far from glorious, far from noble,
We knew nakedness and shame.

With just one bite I had forfeited all.
At a single stroke was paradise lost.
In attempt to be equal to my God
I hadn't stopped to count the cost.

Since it conflicted with my desire,
I believed God's truth to be a lie.
But truth is truth, believed or not,
And truth had said that I would die.

Though in my body I'd live on,
Not queen of Eden, but farmer's wife,
My spirit died—that link to God.
And where spirit dies, there is no life.

There's a reason for my telling, friend.
There are some things you need to see.
Take heed and learn the lessons well,
For you stand to lose as much as me.

The serpent's lies have never changed
Through all his time upon this land.
His plan remains the same as then:
To keep you from our Father's hand.

He is bent on your destruction.
Make no mistake, that is his goal.
Deception, lies and tempting words
Are weapons formed against your soul.

He will tell you that there is no sin,
No consequence for wrong behavior.
Because once you think there is no sin,
You'll have no need of any Savior.

He'll whisper to any who will listen
That God is what the weak require,
And the Word of God's a list of rules
To keep you from all you desire.

"You can stand alone without a god
And live this life to the full!" he'll say.
But this life lasts for just a moment,
With eternity ahead to pay.

To serve no god is not an option.
Our only choice is who it's to be.
Will you serve the God of all creation
Or serve the serpent in the tree?

And as you exercise the freedom
To choose the road that you will take,
May you consider these few words
I offer you for caution's sake:

All that's lovely is not good.
All that's pleasant is not best.
All that's offered should not be taken.
All that's counseled is not blessed.

Know the source of what you hold.
Know the way your road will go.
And bring your questions to the Lord;
For to whom you listen, you will follow.

Just as the choice made long ago
As I stood before the serpent's tree,
The choices you will make today
Will echo through eternity.

Reflection: After the Fall

When their relationship with God had been damaged by disobedience, Adam and Eve's relationship with each other suffered also. When God confronted Adam about eating from the forbidden tree, Adam was ready to sacrifice Eve—blaming her before God for the sin. (Hey! What happened to "bone of my bone & flesh of my flesh" in Genesis 2:23?) The knowledge of good & evil was now applied *to her and to God*.

Genesis 3:12—"the woman You put here with me, she gave me some fruit from the tree."

Also—Eve was not given a name until after the fall! Until then she was called "woman" because she was taken from man (bone of my bone, etc.). They were part of each other—together, each half of the whole. After the fall, Adam names her Eve. She is now separate, unto herself, apart. She has her own name, her own destiny. They are now two.

Today in our marriage ceremonies we often use the phrase "and the two shall become one", recalling that perfect bond, that perfect oneness relationship that was present in the garden before the fall. And the woman, generally speaking, takes the last name of the man. Why? I think maybe it's because we inherently yearn for that kind of relationship—yearn to be man and wo-man. But marriage is a constant challenge, for both must wrestle with that knowledge of what the other should be or do—what is "good" and what is "evil" as each sees it.

The tree is still there.

This was a very difficult poem to write. The story itself is fraught with difficulty. Bad things happening to good people, God allowing it to happen. But the lesson is important. We need to hear what it's saying.

The Story of Job

Romans 8:35,37

Who shall separate us from the love of Christ? Shall trouble or hardship or persecution or famine or nakedness or danger or sword? . . . No, in all these things we are more than conquerors through him who loved us.

Around the royal seat of heaven
A gathering of angels bowed,
And from His throne the King could see
That Satan stood within the crowd.

Now it is that spirit's driving goal
To force a wedge 'tween God and man
To destroy the tie of Father to son
And erase God's image from the land.

What brought him to this hallowed place?
What business had he with the King?
And when a hush fell o'er the host
God spoke, and asked where he had been.

"Roaming through Your sad creation,"
The traitor smiled as he replied,
"Among Your master works on earth -
Filled with evil, sin and pride.

The very fruit of Your own hand
Rejects Your law and scorns Your ways.
They wallow in their decadence
And other gods receive their praise.

Judgment should be swift and sure
For evil reigns throughout that globe!
A *holy* god would not forebear!"
"But," said God, "have you seen Job?"

"Job?" the evil angel spat!
"A man who lives a life of ease
Surrounded by what You provide?
Of course the man would strive to please!

He serves the One who gives him wealth.
He uses goodness as a tool.
His worship oils the course of blessing.
It only proves he's not a fool!

But remove Your guarding hand today,
Stop the flow of wealth and grace,
And tomorrow his allegiance ends
And he will curse You to Your face!

No man serves You out of love!
There is no worship without greed.
They raise their hands so You will fill them.
It's not who You are—it's what they need."

"Very well," said God to Satan,
"All he has is in your hands.
Do with it what you desire,
But lay not a finger on the man."

Permission granted, he left the hall,
A triumphant grin upon his face,
To plot the evil he would do
To the unsuspecting man of grace.

In a single hour disaster fell,
More than one could hope to stand,
For everything that good man had
Was ripped abruptly from his hand.

One by one in quick procession
Servants came to the house of Job,
And each reported tragedy
Of robbers, fire, wind and foes.

All his worldly goods were gone.
His sons and daughters now lay dead.
He tore his robe in stunned despair
And sat with dust upon his head.

"I came with nothing to this world
And with nothing I shall leave.
The Lord both gives and takes away."
And he worshipped in the midst of grief.

Again the scene in Heaven played
As Satan entered God's domain.
Defeated in his first attempt
He sought once more to prove his claim.

"Have you considered Job," asked God,
"How he maintains integrity,
Though smitten through no fault of his
For reasons that he cannot see?"

"Skin for skin!" rejoined the foe.
"Your hand still guards his flesh and bones!
The trial is yet incomplete,
For I've only touched the things he owns."

So God ordered that Job's life be spared,
Withdrawing His protection now.
And the upright man was quickly struck
By painful sores from feet to brow.

"Are you still holding on to virtue
After this?" Job's wife decried,
Watching as he scraped his sores.
"Why not just curse God and die!"

"Your words are foolish," he replied.
"Should we not accept what will befall,
Whether it be good or ill?
For God is author of it all."

Then came four good men to Job,
Friends who sorrowed when they heard.
They sat with him to show support,
And for seven days said not a word.

Then from the silence Job cried out
And cursed the day that he was born!
Longed for death that would not come
For an end to pain and loss and scorn.

The four friends heard in shocked dismay
The dreadful words of Job's lament,
Until the first could not refrain
From putting forth his argument.

"You who strengthened feeble hands,
Whose wisdom helped the weak ones learn,
Can you not discern the truth
Now that the tables have been turned?

Trouble springs not from earth
Nor hardship from a fallow ground -
Unless the seeds of sin were sown
Unless unrighteousness be found!

It is for good God wounds you now!
Do not despise His discipline.
He injures but will also heal,
If you will just appeal to Him.

Lay your cause before His feet.
Confess your sin and He shall hear.
He will release you from this torment.
Forgiven ones have naught to fear."

"Have you no pity?" Job cried out,
"Do you now dare to condescend?
Not only has trouble stolen all,
But now it's made a judge out of a friend!

You were kind enough when all was well,
You thought of me as righteous then!
Now that all I had is gone,
You accuse me of some grievous sin.

You must find me guilty, I suppose,
So that your mind will not be vexed;
For if evil falls on righteous ones
You could possibly be next!

God, what is man that you should notice?
That You should lay your hand on him?
Will You never look away from me?
What have I done to You, oh watcher of men?

You probe for fault and search for sin,
Though I'm guiltless in Your sight.
You come at me wave after wave,
While the wicked smile with health and might."

And then the second friend spoke out,
"Your words bluster as the wind!
Would you accuse God with injustice?
With striking those who have not sinned?

History tells us what is true -
God won't reject a blameless man.
The godless perish without hope;
The righteous flourish in His plan."

"But what is good in God's eyes?" asked Job.
"Goodness is nothing in His sight.
He destroys what is evil and what is good.
Both are victims of His might.

Can I demand an explanation,
From the One who shakes the earth?
Whose hands have formed my very bones?
Who can slay the stars or give them birth?

How can I contend with God?
What is the use of trying then?
Who will ask Him, *'What are You doing??'*
And live to see the sun again?"

"Idle talk!" the third friend cried.
"Talk that brings His wrath to flame!
Your trouble's less than you deserve!
Your words and thoughts will bring you shame!

Would you rather God be guilty?
Would you declare our God unfair?
So that you could be His victim
And the evil His to bear?"

Again and again the friends spoke out
Declaring what Job must have done,
Pronouncing that he earned his woe,
Portraying him a guilty one.

Again and again Job fought their words,
Would not accept guilt from their hand.
For if God weighed with honest scales,
He'd be found a faithful man.

Then came a voice that silenced all,
For God Himself spoke loud and clear.
"Brace yourself, Job, for I shall be
The one to ask the questions here!

Who laid the footings of the earth?
Who set the boundaries of the seas?
Were you there for life's creation?
Stand up now and answer me!

Can you dispatch the lightening bolts?
Can you touch a cloud and call for rain?
Did you give the horse its awesome strength
Or clothe his neck with a flowing mane?

Do you know the way to the abode of light?
Do you know where the dark resides?
Did you cause the sun to shine?
Or set the schedule for the tides?"

Heaven's master declared His rule,
That what He says shall be fulfilled
In all of heaven and all of earth,
Of all that happened, of all that will.

This was the one Almighty God,
And yet He called Job by his name!
He knew about all the things that happened
He knew his trouble and his pain.

Though Job's questions went unanswered
And he received no reason for his woe,
He heard from the God who is over all!
And that was enough for him to know.

Then God rebuked in a mighty voice
The men who had admonished Job,
Who accused him wrongfully of sin,
Speaking of things they did not know.

And then God asked His servant man
To give the one thing that remained
Of all his possessions of all he had -
A prayer for the friends who did defame.

Job gave that only thing he had
And prayed for the men who caused him grief.
Then God restored all that was lost
To the man who did not yield belief.

A righteous man beset by trouble
For reasons he could not explore,
Wrestled with his faith and pain
And in the process found his Lord.

We will seldom know the reasons
Of why trouble comes our way,
Why bad things happen to those we love,
Why unfairness sometimes rules our days.

But if we wrestle with our God
Exposing questions, doubts and fears,
The process reaps its own reward
By connecting us to the One who hears.

It just may have to be enough
To know He's with us in the fray,
That be it here or later on
There will be a better day.

And what a joyful thought that the God of all,
When faith on earth is in decline,
Would point to me with a Father's pride . . .
"Have you considered *this* child of mine?"

The day after the crucifixion. What was it like for the followers of Jesus?

Reflection:
The Children of Saturday

That Saturday, the day after the crucifixion, must have been a terrible day for the disciples of Jesus. On Friday, their focus was on Jesus and His horrible torture and death. But on Saturday, I think the focus would have been on themselves, and what life would hold without Him. All the questions, all the doubts, all the uncertainties, all the grief.

Just a few days before, all seemed clear to them. Now what do they do? Can they go back to catching fish, or collecting taxes or selling cloth? That life would hold nothing for them anymore, not after what they had seen and participated in for three years. They had seen the lame walk, the blind see, the dead rise, thousands fed with a couple loaves and fishes, thousands hailing Jesus as King and Messiah on the road to Jerusalem. They had sat with Him, learned from Him, called Him friend, rabbi and Lord. They were now left with only the memories of His teachings, without the reality, the support of His presence. They were nobodies to the rest of the world, important and unique only in His world. They must have felt like their own lives were lost on that cross. Now all they could do was go home and salvage what they could from what they had left behind, hearing only the echoes of words and ideas of last year or last week. They did not anticipate the Resurrection, had no conception of the Holy Spirit. This was only Saturday.

Sometimes it seems to me that our country is there—stuck in a Saturday of our own making. Our land was founded by people looking to worship God and live their lives with Him at the center. To them, God was alive and present—a reality.

But today, in large part, we are the children of Saturday—a Saturday generation. It's as if Sunday hasn't happened. There is

66

the vague memory of the teachings of Jesus (the "Judeo-Christian ethic") but somewhere along the road the reality of it has died. We (our country in general) are not seeking or living our lives by the power of a living Jesus, and so there isn't the support and certainty that comes with His presence. The focus is on ourselves and how to live life without Him. We've gone back to catching fish and selling cloth and collecting taxes, the faint echoes of His teachings bringing confusion and frustration. We now live with the stress and angst and mental gymnastics it takes to live in a world where we are nobodies—important and unique only in a world we no longer seek and touch—His Kingdom.

The story of Jonah is not a simple child's story of a guy who got swallowed by a whale. Jonah was a complicated character who knew God, but vehemently disagreed with His plan. It's a tale of the struggle between our will and God's plan.

The Story of Jonah

Isaiah 55:8

For my thoughts are not your thoughts, neither are your ways my ways.

"Is it right for you to be angry?"
And immediately came the defiant reply:
"Yes!" said the prophet to his God.
"And I am angry enough to die!"

This man had been rescued from certain death!
Had helped change the fate of an entire city!
You'd think he'd rejoice at these miraculous things,
But he was filled with anger and self-pity.

What could have caused this radical response?
Why be bitter when so many were saved?
Why shake a fist in the face his Lord,
And choose to take his anger to the grave?

Well—to go back, this mission from the start
Was to Jonah an anathema,
For he was to bring a word of warning
To the detested people of Nineveh.

For years he had taken God's word to men.
Untold miles he had gladly trod.
But he resolved that this time would be different.
He would run from this message and from his God.

He could not, would not do the task
His God required that he do.
There was no sense, no rightness in it,
To warn them of wrath that was overdue.

The people of Nineveh were evil, brutal.
It was justice that was required, not pity!
And he refused to be the one
To say the words that could save that city.

Jonah would obey his own sense of right.
He would sound no alarm, not let it be known.
There will be no prophet, no time to repent.
And those people will reap what they had sown.

What if, warned, they turned to God?
Would He then erase all they've done?
If they pay a vow to avoid destruction
It does not make them Abraham's sons!

So, to a ship in the seaport of Joppa
The prophet Jonah made his way,
Not sailing *to* but sailing *from*
The greatest mission of his day.

He bought the ticket for his journey.
(But the total cost was yet to ensue.)
And on a ship bound for a distant shore
Went the prodigal prophet of the Jews.

Once out upon the open sea,
A storm so violent, so severe
Threatened to destroy the ship,
And the seasoned crew was filled with fear.

With the wind howling and the water raging,
They dumped their cargo into the sea!
And each cried out to his god to save them,
While Jonah was down below—asleep.

"Get up!" the captain yelled to the prophet.
"How can you sleep with all this chaos?
Whatever god it is that you serve -
Pray to it now that all won't be lost!"

And feeling that this deadly storm
Was brought by a god for some evil done,
The crew cast lots to reveal the guilty,
And it fell on Jonah to be the one.

"Why have you brought this trouble on us?"
"Who are you and where are you from?"
"Who is your god and what is your offense?"
"Make it right, or we all are undone!"

"I am a Hebrew, a prophet of God,
The God of Heaven who made land and sea.
And I boarded this ship to run away
From the mission He had given me."

"What??" The astounded crew responded.
"You serve a god with so much power?
You must be mad to run from Him!
We'll all be dead within the hour!"

"Throw me overboard," said Jonah.
"The sea will calm and the storm will cease.
I am the one who brought this danger;
Be rid of me and there shall be peace."

But the sailors were loath to carry that out.
They feared his God would avenge this man.
So they tried in vain to row to safety,
But had at last to abandon the plan.

"Throw me over and save yourselves!
I don't want you to die," was Jonah's plea.
So they cried to God not to find them at fault,
And threw him into the raging sea.

The astonished sailors watched in awe
As *instantly* the storm was quelled!
So they worshiped this new and mighty God
For the miracle they had beheld.

While Jonah, sinking into the sea,
To the silent depths of a watery grave,
With seaweed wrapped around his head,
Felt his life quickly ebbing away.

But God had other plans for him.
A second chance to obey and grow.
A second chance to see that God's grace
Is greater, more powerful than he had known.

He provided a fish to swallow Jonah,
And keep him alive for the next three days.
(It's something people find hard to believe;
But when Almighty God speaks, creation obeys!)

From inside the fish Jonah thanked his God.
He raised his voice and vowed anew
To make good on his pledge to follow Him,
And do what God would have him do.

The Lord then commanded this uncommon fish
To vomit Jonah onto dry land.
And the word of the Lord came again to the prophet:
"Go warn the Ninevites"—the original plan.

Obedient but grudging, Jonah went to that city,
Hoping they'd ignore the warning he brought.
He did not want to witness their salvation.
God might forgive them—Jonah would not!

Ninevites did not deserve forgiveness -
It was obvious to see for anyone.
And no matter what they said or did now,
It could never make up for all they'd done.

When news of the prophesy reached their king
That destruction would come in forty days,
He put off his robe and called for a fast,
And the people repented and they prayed.

Their response was swift and city-wide,
As they looked to God, prayed it wasn't too late.
Their repentance was real, but they did not know
If deliverance or destruction would be their fate.

Jonah, angry and distraught,
Sat on a hill overlooking the city.
He wanted to witness his enemy's ruin,
But had a front row seat of God's grace and pity.

As he sat on the hill in the heat of the day,
The sun beating down was merciless.
The Lord then caused a gourd plant to grow
To give him shade and ease his distress.

Jonah was very happy for the plant
That kept the sun from off his head.
But when he awoke the very next day
He found the gourd withered and dead.

And that is why, at the start of our tale,
Jonah wished to die in his chagrin.
He knew that God had killed that plant,
And he sensed that redemption was in the wind.

"You wanted the gourd to live," said God
"This one soulless plant you did not create.
But all those people down that hill are mine.
Should I not care for their eternal fate?"

But Jonah could not put aside his feelings.
"God's making a mistake," was his surmise.
"The people down that hill weren't worthy of grace.
Their offences called for their demise."

God tried to reason with this prophet he loved,
Tried to break through the bitter crust of the man.
He did not want simply mindless obedience,
But duty that rises from a trust in His plan.

The Lord wanted his prophet Jonah to see
That there was here a basic truth to be learned:
That mercy is not mercy if there is no offence,
And grace is not grace if it can be earned.

God accepted the repentance of the Ninevites,
And tens of thousands were saved that day.
But there was no joy on the top of the hill
Where the man who helped make it possible stayed.

So what happened with Jonah? What came next?
Were God's words to him useless, or did he finally see?
Did the prophet return to his home, dejected -
Or did he run down the hill and rejoice in the city?

We are not told the choice that Jonah made,
If he then walked with God, or walked away.
The choice was his alone to make.
Either way, his life would be changed that day.

This struggle will be fought for as long as men live,
When God's plan is contrary to our own will.
This choice is ours alone to make:
To rejoice in the city . . . or to sit on the hill.

Do you desire God's favor in your life? What is it? What does it look like? How do we get it?

Reflection: The Favor of God

I thought favor meant an extended time, or even a lifetime, of blessing from God with difficulties at a minimum. If God's favor was upon someone, I thought that he or she would be successful in their spiritual, personal and outward life—an obvious resting of God's blessing. I was wrong.

Luke 1:30—"Do not be afraid, Mary, you have found favor with God. . . . . . ."

Luke 2:52—"And Jesus grew in wisdom and stature, and in favor with God and men."

Acts 7:45—". . . David, who enjoyed God's favor . . . "

These are the only people said to have God's "favor" in the Bible. (according to the NIV)

Mary did not fit my picture of favor. Of course, giving birth to and raising Jesus was a tremendous gift. But her life looked very difficult. Unwed, pregnant, the stress must have been tremendous. Poor. Giving birth in a stable. Watching her son being tortured, reviled and killed. It was not my idea of "favor".

David's life was filled with war. His son turned against him, humiliating him before all the people. Again, not my idea of favor.

Jesus did not fit my assumption. Too much suffering.

After more studying, it now appears to me that favor is: *God enabling us to do His will, to further His Kingdom.* "Favor" is what is needed, spiritually and/or materially and/or emotionally to do the job. It is not purposeless benevolence. It isn't bestowing favor to make life better. God knows that our joy and satisfaction in life comes with our flowing in His plan—*but our joy is an effect, not the purpose for His favor.*

Then I found that favor has the same root word that can be translated as blessing, grace, mercy. *They all have a purpose.* We were not saved only so that we could be happy with God in Heaven. That is a result, but there is more to it. We were saved to further His Kingdom, to bring others to Him, to establish and display, so far as we are able, His love and His principles in all the areas of our lives so that others will be drawn to Him—so that they, too, can share in the joy and fulfillment of knowing Him here and now and through eternity.

We use the words "blessing from God" too glibly. If we truly believe that something is a blessing from God, or if we believe that we are experiencing God's favor, then we need to find out how He wants us to use it. Because it comes not only with joy, but with a purpose beyond ourselves.

An Essay: Up From the Valley

"Yea, though I walk through the valley of the shadow of death, I will fear no evil for You are with me. Your rod and Your staff they comfort me."

Being in "the valley" is a condition of the soul. It's a difficult place to be. It might be a valley of grief or heartache, or illness, or financial trouble or one of broken relationships. As these things come into our lives we begin to lose our trust in God, pull away from the church and people, and step by step we enter our valley. It's much more serious than "the blues" because we add God to the equation and still come up with no answer. In the valley we begin to believe that God doesn't care about our situation.

The first three words of this section are "Yea, though I".

It's not "Yea, though WE". The valley is a solitary place, even if we are in the situation with someone else. No one can climb into our heart and head and understand how we feel. Our thoughts and our feelings are uniquely our own. Others can point us on a right path or weep with us or pray for us or cheer us on, but they do not "know". We can't expect them to.

But God knows. The Bible says that God knows the number of hairs on our heads! In other words, He knows the minutest possible thing about us—something that changes moment to moment. No one, not even ourselves, know that. God told us that in His Word because He wants us to understand that *he really does "know"*. And He wouldn't bother to know, if He didn't also care.

In our valleys, we are alone—with God, who knows how we feel.

"Yea though I walk through"

We're supposed to be walking through, not setting up camp! God doesn't want us to stay there in the valley. He doesn't want us to move in with someone who lives there! Ever meet people who are perpetually in a valley—sad, pessimistic, awfulizing and catastrophizing people who seem to take comfort and identity within their valley, camouflaging bitterness with a victimhood? Don't move in with them! Don't share that kind of conversation, the playing and replaying of difficulties and resignation to bad feelings. We need to keep walking.

But valleys are places with fog, obscuring our vision, keeping us from seeing clearly. And we're hurting, and maybe we can't even find the path. How can we move? Where do we walk? King David knew.

Reading the Psalms, we see that David consistently wrote about being in a valley. He knew what it was like, was many times in distress, almost to the point of despair. Then, after describing the horrible place of discouragement and fear, in the next verse he's praising and worshiping God! Was David a scitzo? Did his emotions do a complete about-face? No. *He found the secret to getting out of the valley. He plodded though, kept walking, by acknowledging who God is—Almighty Creator, Counselor, King, Lord—in spite of his distress.* He did that because his distress, his circumstance didn't diminish who God is. I know you don't feel like praising God in the valley. I get that. But it takes an act of the will—aside from, and in spite of, feelings. David said, "I WILL praise Him . . ." it was a decision, not a feeling.

"the valley of the shadow of death"

You see, this isn't the valley of death, only the *shadow* of death. It has the form of death, the feeling of it perhaps, but there is no substance. How can I say that? Because in order to have a shadow you must have light. *Jesus is the Light.* He is there, and He is *life*, not death. And if we are looking to Him, toward Him (the Light), the shadows will be behind us! The awfulness of our circumstances won't be in our face, it won't be in the forefront of our thoughts. Then the weight of it all, the overwhelmingness of it all (the *death* of it all) will fall away because we're choosing to look at the Light, at hope.

"His rod and His staff comfort me"

Do you suppose, or have you been told, that the rod and the staff are for discipline? That's wrong! A shepherd's staff or rod is not for beating the sheep. It can gently nudge a sheep to go in the right direction. But mostly it's a walking stick—a crutch. It's there to comfort us as we walk through the valley. We can lean on it. Whatever form it takes, it is pieces of gace and mercy. An encouraging word, or a bit of good news, or just a bright sunny day that warms our heart—we can lean on that crutch, that piece of grace, that helps us keep on walking out of that valley.

I need to tell you that I know what a valley experience is. I'm not talking though my hat, speaking of things I haven't experienced. I had a wonderful, sweet, often very ill, wheelchair-bound daughter who died at 17. I've lost a home to foreclosure, I've lost a much loved job, been betrayed by friends, divorced after 34 years of marriage. I know valleys. And I know there's a way out.

The Bible says, "In all things give thanks." Not "FOR all things give thanks." We don't have to thank God for bad things—*He* didn't send them to us, it's just a part of living in this world. As long as we're here there will be valleys. We just have to think of something—anything—to praise Him for, to thank Him for. Praise Him for the splendor of creation. Worship Him because He spoke and things came into being. Praise Him for the beauty of a newborn baby or the petals of a flower. Worship Him because He is the almighty and eternal God. Thank Him because He sent His Son to die for us.

And with each word of worship we speak, and with each word of praise we say out loud, with each phrase of thanksgiving, we take a step on the path that leads out of the valley.

Don't feel like it? That's okay. You're emotions aren't in it? That's okay. That's why the Bible calls it the *sacrifice* of praise. Do it anyway. I can tell you from experience that step by step, praise by praise, thanks by thanks, you will get above the fog, and you will be able to see clearly again, and you will find yourself on the mountainside, on a path that just keeps leading up higher.

Keep walking. The view gets much better!